THIS MINECRAFT BOOK BELONGS TO:

NAME:
....

MY AGE:

MY FAVOURITE MINECRAFT MOB IS:

- ○ ENDERMAN
- ○ SKELETON
- ○ PIG
- ○ CREEPER
- ○ CHICKEN
- ○ ZOMBIE

MY FAVOURITES!

GAME:
....

MOVIE:
....

TV SHOW:
....

BOOK:
....

MUSIC:
....

ANIMAL:
....

FOOD:
....

DRINK:
....

COLOUR:
....

Published by D.C. Thomson & Co.,Ltd 185 Fleet Street, London EC4A 2HS. © D.C. Thomson, 2023. Whilst every reasonable care will be taken neither D.C. Thomson & Co.,Ltd., nor its agents accept liability for loss or damage to colour transparencies or any other material submitted to this publication. Distributed by Frontline Ltd, Stuart House, St John's St, Peterborough, Cambridgeshire PE1 5DD. Tel: +44 (0) 1733 555161. Website: www.frontlinedistribution. co.uk. EU Representative Office: DC Thomson & Co Ltd, c/o Findmypast Ireland, Irishtown, Athlone, Co. Westmeath, N37 XP52

DC THOMSON EXPORT DISTRIBUTION (excluding AU and NZ) Seymour Distribution Ltd, 2 East Poultry Avenue, London EC1A 9PT Tel: +44(0)20 7429 4000 Fax: +44(0)20 7429 4001 Website: www.seymour.co.uk

Enquiries: editor@110gaming.com

DRAW A SKIN!

Summer or winter themed?

How about a spooky Halloween skin?

Rep your fave game or movie!

THE HISTORY OF

■ Before they decided on Minecraft, the game was almost called Cave Game or The Order of the Stone! At the start, Steve was the only mob and there were only three blocks!

DID YOU KNOW?

THE TITLE THE ORDER OF THE STONE WAS REUSED IN MINECRAFT: STORY MODE!

■ The game was officially released! To celebrate, The End was added to the game, along with Endermen and the Ender Dragon!

2009   2010   2011   2012

■ A big year for Minecraft! First, they added Survival Mode, then came Skeletons and Zombies. They rounded off the year by crafting The Nether into the game!

I'M PRETTY SCARY!

■ This was the year of the Pretty Scary update. On the pretty side, the game came to console. To get the scary, Mojang also added in the Wither!

MINECRAFT

■ Can you believe it took this long before Horses came to Minecraft? It's true! This year also added loads of new Redstone items like the Hopper and Dropper.

■ You could get crafty on the go with Minecraft Earth! This AR mobile game introduced exclusive new mobs as well as a totally immersive new way to play.

2013   2014   2019   2020

■ Move over Steve, it's Alex's time to shine! The new character also brought loads of new biomes and the Chicken Jockey mob with them!

■ Another new spin-off brought us the awesome top-down dungeon crawler, Minecraft Dungeons. With loads of incredible new mobs and characters, plenty of epic environments to explore and a whole new approach to the gameplay, Dungeons has been a welcome addition to the Minecraft family.

■ **NEW GAME ALERT!**

MINECRAFT LEGENDS OUT NOW!

DID YOU KNOW?

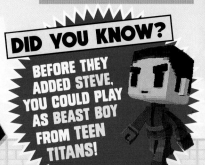

BEFORE THEY ADDED STEVE, YOU COULD PLAY AS BEAST BOY FROM TEEN TITANS!

MINECRAFT Legends

LOOK INSIDE!

Get ready to see a brand new side of Minecraft!

PIGLIN INVASION

■ The Piglins are invading from The Nether, and the people and monsters of The Overworld will need to team up to defend their homes! Are you the mighty hero that can bring them together?

GRAND STRATEGY

■ Minecraft Legends is an action-strategy game that is really different to the regular Minecraft you're used to! In this one, you'll command squads of animal allies, recruit scary monsters to your side, fight the Piglin hordes and build massive army bases!

MINECRAFT SPIN-OFFS!

There are other Minecraft-related adventures! Have you played them?

MINECRAFT: STORY MODE   2015

■ Minecraft: Story Mode is a point-and-click adventure game that feels like a TV show! Can Jesse save the world from evil with The Order of the Stone?

MINECRAFT STORY MODE

PLAYED IT! ✓

SUPER SMASH BROS. ULTIMATE   2018

■ Steve, Alex and the world of Minecraft are all in Super Smash Bros. Ultimate thanks to Challenger Pack 7!

PLAYED IT! ✓

MOUNT UP

■ In this adventure, you'll be able to tame and ride on all sorts of wild creatures from around The Overworld! We're hoping we can swim around on a big Axolotl.

CO-OP CAPER

■ You can play all of Minecraft Legends in co-op with up to three friends over the internet, which means that warriors won't have to take the Piglin threat on alone!

XBOX GAME PASS

■ Right from the release day, Minecraft Legends has been available to play on Xbox Game Pass at no extra cost — what a bargain!

MINECRAFT DUNGEONS
2020

■ Defeat the Arch-Illager with up to three friends in this action packed, loot-filled dungeon crawler!

MINECRAFT DUNGEONS

PLAYED IT! ✓

HYTALE
TBA

■ Popular Minecraft custom game server Hypixel is becoming its own game! While not an official spin-off, Hytale still has lots in common with Minecraft.

HYTALE

PLAYED IT! ✓

MINECRAFT Legends

MEET THE MOBS

YOU'LL NEED TO GET SOME MOBS ON YOUR SIDE TO BEAT THE EVIL PIGLINS!

SKELETON

These sharp shooters are great at long range attacks. They're ready to fight anytime thanks to their sturdy helmets – just keep them away from lava!

LOL!

What musical instruments do Skeletons play?

TROM-BONES!

COBBLESTONE GOLEMS

Cobblestone Golems can pack a punch! They're so tough that when they attack, it won't take long for their target to fall.

GRINDSTONE GOLEM

When battles start feeling a bit too chaotic, you can count on Grindstone Golems to knock over entire groups of Piglins!

CREEPER

Don't run from hissing sounds, find where it's coming from! Once you've got Creepers on side, you can build their spawner to summon them for battles.

WHO WOULD YOU TEAM UP WITH?

....

PIGLIN PATHFINDER

CHOOSE THE RIGHT PATH TO LEAD YOUR ARMY INTO BATTLE!

YOU DID IT!

TOP TIP!

Support Zombies with extra fire power or a Mossy Golem for a boost in battle!

MOSSY GOLEMS

These softies won't attack a Piglin or their structures, but they're still useful allies. Their healing properties lets you and your army keep up the good fight!

PLANK GOLEMS

To guarantee victory, keep these mobs away from the busiest parts of the battlefield. The arrows they shoot are only aimed at Piglins!

ZOMBIE

Zombies can take a hit and are happy to charge into battle first! They aren't invincible and will need back up.

LEGENDARY PUZZLES!

BEAT THESE PUZZLES TO DEFEAT THE PIGLINS AND ESCAPE THE NETHER!

CROSS-SWORD!

■ Prove that you're the hero the Overworld needs by completing this tricky crossword!

ACROSS

- **4** This is where you start in Minecraft
- **6** These mobs walk on their hind legs
- **8** These guys created Minecraft

DOWN

- **1** A second dimension in Minecraft
- **2** A weapon that can be used to slice
- **3** These cubes are used for building
- **5** A green creature that explodes
- **7** Our fave new spin-off
- **8** A creature in the Minecraft world

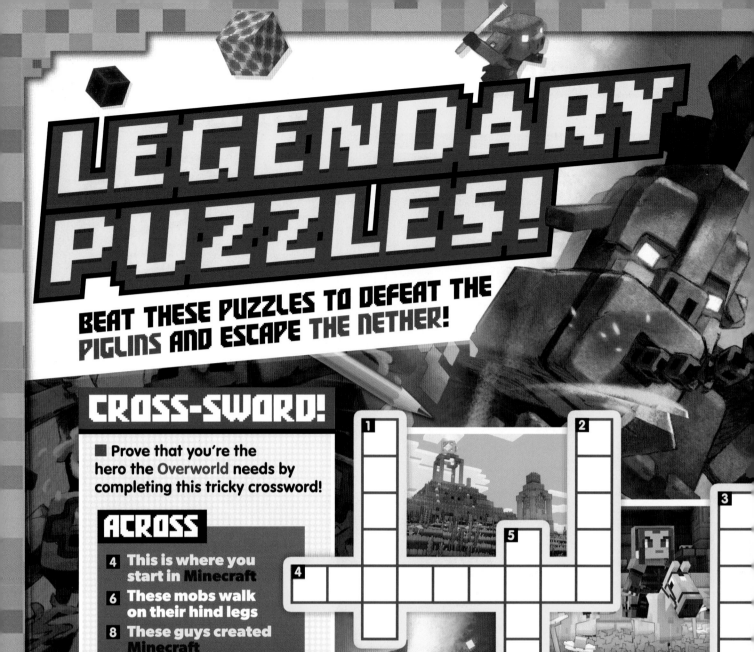

ODD ONE OUT!

■ Four Piglins stand before you... but which one is the odd one out?!

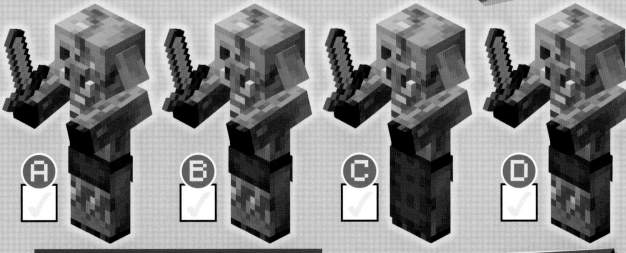

A ✓
B ✓
C ✓
D ✓

The Piglins are planning to invade the Overworld! Could you be the hero that stops them in Minecraft Legends?

ESCAPE THE NETHER!

■ You're trapped in The Nether! Can you find the correct path and return to the Overworld?

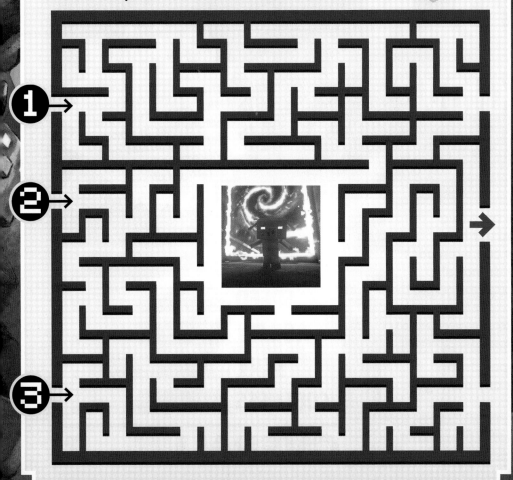

1 →
2 →
3 →

YOU MADE IT!

13

POWER PROFILE!

POWER UP!

Out of all the mobs in Minecraft, the Warden has the highest health and dishes out the highest melee damage!

WARDEN

DID YOU KNOW?

⭐ Wardens can only be found in Deep Dark biomes, and they burst out from under the ground when they're alerted by Sculk Shriekers!

⭐ You don't need to be next to a Warden for it to hurt you – it has a ranged sonic boom that can even pass through blocks to inflict damage!

⭐ Even although this mob looks huge, it can squeeze into small spaces to chase you through narrow corridors.

⭐ Not only are they super-strong, but Wardens don't take any damage from lava or fire!

⭐ Vibrations, smells and any contact with players can all make the Warden angry, and if this anger builds up, it'll attack!

DAMAGE ALERT!

The Warden can't see! This completely blind creature lives in darkness and uses smells and vibrations to detect nearby players.

STATS:

STRENGTH	
SPEED	
AGILITY	
SKILL	
COOLNESS	

OVERALL ⟫⟫⟫ 7

COMICCRAFT

DAVE

MAX

MINNIE & CRAFTY

GET READY FOR SOME MINI MINECRAFT LOLS WITH MAX, DAVE, CRAFTY AND MINNIE!

LOCKED OUT!

Argh! I've lost my keys!

I just passed some keys — I can show you where!

Woah, best neighbour achievement unlocked!

There you go!

GROAN

EASTER EGGS!

Aww, look! The Easter Bunny's left us loads of Easter eggs!

Erm... I'm not so sure...

CRACK! CRACK!

Uh oh...

That's *eggsactly* what we didn't want!

SPRING CLEAN!

Ew, Dave! Do you ever tidy up?

Maybe it's time for a spring clean?

A spring clean? Hmm... That gives me an idea!

Who knew cleaning could be so fun!

BOING! BOING!

15

BEST EVER MOBS!

TEAM 110'S FAVOURITE MINECRAFT MOBS – WILL YOUR FAVOURITES MAKE THE CUT?

CREEPER

■ Creepers are the A-listers of the Minecraft mob world – everything they do, they do with a bang!

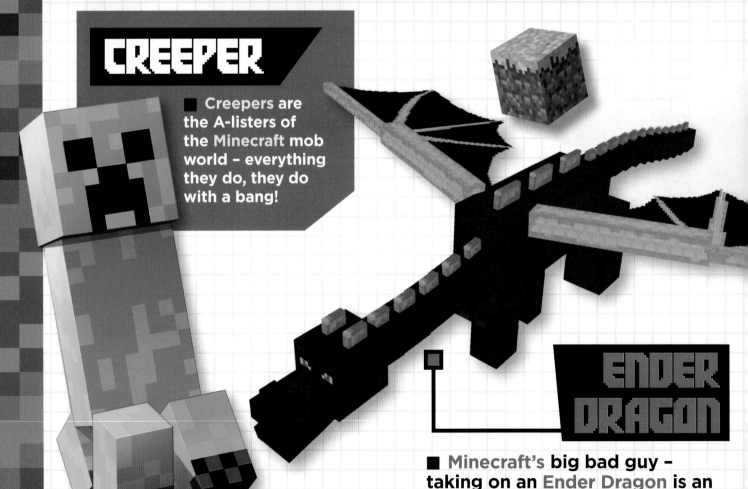

ENDER DRAGON

■ Minecraft's **big bad guy** – taking on an **Ender Dragon** is an intense challenge that no other mob can match!

WOLF

■ Taming a Wolf is one of the most rewarding and fun things you can do in Minecraft. Who wouldn't want a furry friend following them around?!

SNOW GOLEM

■ If only we could build a Snow Golem in real life, that would be so awesome! You could have fun snowball fights every day!

PIG

■ We used to think **Pigs** made for really tasty snacks, but after **Reuben** from **Story Mode** we're always gonna have a soft spot for these little guys!

ENDERMEN

■ **Endermen** are super-scary! These neutral mobs from **The End** have the ability to teleport, and will only attack when a player looks them in the eyes!

ARE YOU LOOKING AT ME?!

I HAVE THE BIGGEST HOOTER IN THE VILLAGE!

VILLAGER

■ **Villagers** are strange-looking guys that are cool to hang out with and trade. Plus, anyone who manages to look cool with a nose like that gets our vote!

SPIDER JOCKEY

■ **Spider Jockeys** are crazy – FACT! They are literally bow and arrow-wielding **Skeletons** that ride giant **Spiders** – that's 100% bonkers!

WITHER

■ **Withers** are immune to fire, lava, drowning and suffocation and don't get hurt by their own explosions – terrifying!

BLIMEY! YOU'RE PRETTY HEAVY FOR A SKELETON, MATE!

MOOSHROOM

■ **Mooshrooms** are weird and that's why we like them! We love the fact that they produce mushroom stew when they're milked!

MOB MAKER!

GRAB YOUR PENCILS AND PENS AND CREATE YOUR OWN MOB!

GET MOO-VING!

HERE ARE SOME CLASSIC MOBS FOR INSPO!

WRITE YOUR MOB'S NAME AND TYPE HERE!

NAME: ....

TYPE: ....

MINECRAFT JOKES!

I HAD A CONVERSATION WITH A CREEPER ONCE!
HE TOTALLY BLEW MY MINE!

WHAT IS THE NATIONAL SPORT OF MINECRAFT?
BOXING!

HEY CREEPER, HOW WAS THE PARTY?

IT WAS A BLAST!

WHAT'S COBBLESTONE'S FAVOURITE MUSIC?
ROCK MUSIC!

WHAT DID THE MUM DIRT BLOCK SAY TO HER CHILD?
YOU'RE GROUND-ED!

WHY DID THE SQUID CROSS THE OCEAN?
TO GET TO THE OTHER TIDE!

BOY BYE!

WHAT DID STEVE SAY TO HIS GIRLFRIEND?
I DIG YOU!

HOW DOES STEVE GET HIS EXERCISE?

HE RUNS AROUND THE BLOCK!

THE A-Z OF MINECRAFT

FROM ARROWS TO ZOMBIES, EVERYTHING YOU NEED TO KNOW ABOUT MINECRAFT!

A IS FOR ARROW

If an arrow is shot through lava it will be set on fire.

B IS FOR BLOCKS

It wouldn't be Minecraft without the blocky style of the world. Loads of different blocks make up this awesome game!

HISSSSS!

C IS FOR CREEPER

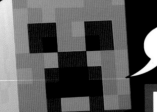

This angry mob is always blowing his top!

D IS FOR DEATH

Death is at every turn in Minecraft and you need to be ready to respawn at a moment's notice! Unless you're in Survival Mode you'll live to mine another day!

E IS FOR EGG

When thrown, an egg has a 1 in 8 chance of spawning a Chick.

F IS FOR FEATHER

Feathers are super handy if you love to embrace your inner archer as you'll need them to craft arrows!

H IS FOR HIDE

With so many dangers in the Minecraft world it's important that you know when to hide and when to run. When an Enderman is around hide your eyes or you'll be in trouble!

WHO ARE YOU CALLING BIG-NOSE?

G IS FOR GLASS

Want to add some cool windows to your builds? Smelt some glass!

I IS FOR IRON GOLEM

Iron Golems can see hostile mobs through walls or through blocks.

THE A-Z OF MINECRAFT

L IS FOR LADDERS

Ladders are so handy in this game and if you're into building tall structures, you'll need these for speedy access to the top!

M IS FOR MOJANG

The company that created Minecraft!

J IS FOR JACK O' LANTERNS

These creepy pumpkin heads are unbelievably useful – you can use them as a light or to build Snow or Iron Golems. Awesome!

REMEMBER TO FLOSS KIDS!

N IS FOR NETHER

The Nether is one of the coolest and scariest places in Minecraft with its rivers of lava, fire pits and scary mobs.

O IS FOR ORE

Ore is a type of block like Coal, Gold, or Diamond, used for mining and crafting.

P IS FOR PORTAL

OMG, we wish portals were real! Imagine how handy it would be to just zap yourself to where you need to go… why can't this be real?

K IS FOR KNIGHT

We love creating knight armour in Minecraft – it looks awesome!

Q IS FOR QUARTZ

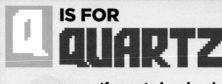

If quartz is mined without a pickaxe, it will drop nothing.

R IS FOR REDSTONE

This was a total game changer for Minecraft. With the introduction of redstone, new inventions and possibilities were unleashed and it's been even more awesome ever since!

THIS TAKES A LOT OF SKULL!

S IS FOR SKELETON

An aggressive mob that attacks with a bow and arrows.

T IS FOR TORCHES

If you're going to go mining, you'll need to torch it up. These are essential for keeping mobs away and marking your route when going underground!

OOPS! I'VE SINGED MY HAIR!

U IS FOR UPDATES

We love when cool new features are added to the game!

V IS FOR VANILLA MINECRAFT

This refers to Minecraft with no texture packs or mods. Vanilla Minecraft is where it all started and it will always be classic!

W IS FOR WOODEN PLANK

One log can be crafted into four wooden planks.

Z IS FOR ZOMBIE

X IS FOR XBOX...

...And PlayStation, PC and tablet. There are so many ways to play Minecraft nowadays whether you're at home or on-the-go – take your world with you, wherever you go!

Y IS FOR YOU

The most important thing about Minecraft is you – the people who create all this awesomeness!

ANYONE FANCY A BACON ROLL?

You'll know these mobs are coming when you hear them grumbling your way, if you're really unlucky it might be the terrifying Zombie Pigmen making an appearance – EEK!

MINECRAFT

MEETS

FORTNITE

THE BATTLE BUS GETS A BLOCKY MAKEOVER IN THIS EPIC MASH-UP!

LOOT LLAMA!

● Fortnite just wouldn't be the same without our fave Loot Llama, so this pixel art version is the perfect decoration for inside the Battle Bus!

WHEEEE!

PREPARE TO LAND!

● It's time to pick your drop zone and get stuck into the action! Where will you land? Nether Shores, Steve Springs, TNT Towers? It's up to you!

WHERE AM I LANDING AGAIN?

PLENTY OF PICKAXES!

● If you're gonna build an epic base, you'll need the right tools for the job. A Battle Bus full of diamond pickaxes ought to do the trick!

SKIN SELECTION!

● There's nothing more rewarding that saving up your V-Bucks for the coolest new skin. Having an on-board armour wardrobe means you can always look the part!

CODEBREAKER!

THESE BLOCKS SPELL OUT THE NAME OF AN AWESOME MINECRAFT MOB! CAN YOU WORK OUT WHAT IT IS?

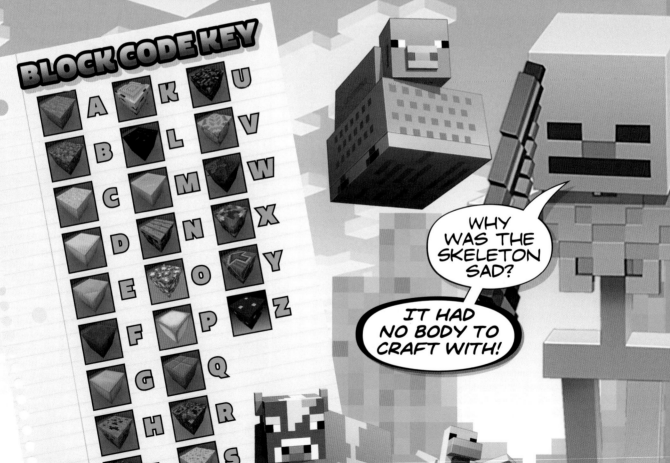

BLOCK BAKE!

MINING IS HUNGRY WORK!

DON'T TRY RECIPES WHERE ALLERGIES MAY BE AN ISSUE.

YOU WILL NEED:

- ☆ 90g Unsalted butter (softened)
- ☆ 280g Rice Krispies
- ☆ TSP Vanilla extract
- ☆ 420g Marshmallows
- ☆ Green food colouring
- ☆ 25g Cocoa powder
- ☆ 125g Chocolate chips

ASK AN ADULT TO HELP!

1 For the top layer, melt 30g butter and 140g marshmallows on a low heat on the hob and stir until smooth. Remove from the heat and add a few drops of green food colouring, vanilla extract, and 140g Rice Krispies.

2 Grease a 9x9 inch square cake tray. Pour in the mixture and smooth with a wooden spoon. Cover with some greaseproof paper and push down gently to even it out to the square shape. Remove the paper and freeze for about an hour.

3 Repeat the first step to make the bottom layer. This time melt 60g butter and 280g marshmallows, then add the cocoa powder and choc chips. Stir until the chips have melted. Remove from the heat and mix in the rest of the cereal.

4 Take the top layer out of the freezer and pour the chocolate mix on top. Place a layer of wax paper over it and even it out with your hands. Remove the paper and pop it back in the freezer for an hour or so to set.

5 Run a knife along the edges of the baking dish to loosen and turn the Krispie block out onto a chopping board. Cut into squares using a knife or a cookie cutter and enjoy!

THAT'S A SQUARE MEAL!

29

NO MOB ZONE!

IT'S TIME TO SHOW THE MOBS WHO'S BOSS!

MOB PHOBIAS!

Check out what these mobs hate the most!

HISSS!

CREEPERS – OCELOTS

These green meanies are super-scared of cats and will run away when they see them!

ZOMBIES – SUN

We've heard of getting sunburn, but Zombies actually catch fire in the daylight – ouch!

ENDERMEN – SNOWBALLS

You won't catch an Enderman in a snowball fight – snowballs are deadly for these guys!

SKELETONS – WOLVES

Everyone knows that dogs love bones, so no wonder Skeletons run away from Wolves!

Turn over for a top trap to boss any mob!

TOP TRAP

REDSTONE

IRON BLOCKS

REDSTO TORCI

1 Create a large pit under where you want to place your trap, then dig out an L-shape in the pit ceiling so that there's a one block layer in between the trap and the pit. Build an Iron Golem in the pit before sealing the ceiling.

TWO MOBS ENTER, ONE MOB LEAVES!

2 Place a sticky piston in the top of the hole then place some redstone diagonally below it. Break a hole in the bottom left corner to create an entrance to the pit.

STICKY PISTON

PUMPKIN

PRESSURE PLATE

3 Place a stone block on top of the hole and add a pressure plate and redstone torch to set the trap. Build a layer of blocks on top of the trap to disguise it, but leave the pressure plate exposed.

TOP TIP!

USE A WOODEN PRESSURE PLATE SO YOU CAN EASILY SEE IT!

4

Wait for a mob to step on the pressure plate then CRASH! They'll fall to the pit where the Iron Golem is waiting! What's great about this trap is that you can safely collect mob drops.

MOB LOLS!

WHAT'S A CREEPER'S FAVE SCHOOL SUBJECT?

HISSSTORY!

HOW DOES A ZOMBIE SAY HELLO?

"PLEASED TO EAT YOU!"

WHY WAS THE ENDER DRAGON CONFUSED BY A BOOK?

IT STARTED AT THE END!

POWER PROFILE!

POWER UP!
Steve has superhuman strength! When you add all the heavy blocks Steve can carry in his inventory, he must be one of the strongest video game characters — EVER!

DAMAGE ALERT!
He might be super-strong, but he still takes damage and gets hungry just like everyone else! If you need Steve in tip-top condition, you need to keep him well-fed!

STEVE

DID YOU KNOW?

⭐ There's a spooky version of Steve! No-one knows if the creepy Herobrine really exists in the game, but we know for sure we wouldn't want to bump into him.

⭐ You can play as Steve and battle it out, Minecraft style, in Super Smash Bros. Ultimate!

⭐ Steve wears the exact same outfit as Zombies! We wonder who wore it first...

⭐ He was the first-ever default Minecraft skin – now there's NINE, including Alex, Noor and Kai!

⭐ You can flip Steve upside-down by renaming the player 'Dinnerbone'!

STATS:

STRENGTH	
SPEED	
AGILITY	
SKILL	
COOLNESS	

OVERALL ⟩⟩⟩ 7.5

COMICCRAFT

DAVE

MAX

MINNIE & CRAFTY

GET READY FOR SOME MINI MINECRAFT LOLS WITH MAX, DAVE, CRAFTY AND MINNIE!

BRIKBLOK

You look so silly!

I'm gonna get so many likes...

This BrikBlok vid will blow up!

GULP

Yup, it's gonna BLOW UP!

PIZZA PRANK!

Let's prank Max and Minnie with this Potion of Invisibility!

We'll hide, then give 'em a fright!

Look Minnie, we've got the place to ourselves!

It worked — they walked right past!

Now for phase 2...

MEANWHILE...

Pee-yew! Did you smell Dave's stinky socks when we came in?

I think he's trying to prank us but don't worry, Minnie...

I've got a prank of my own....

What a shame Dave and Crafty aren't here...

We'll just need to eat ALL this pizza by ourselves!

We're here! We're here!

35

NOT OFFICIAL MINECRAFT PRODUCT. NOT APPROVED BY OR ASSOCIATED WITH MOJANG

76 WAYS TO BOSS THE BLOCKS!

KEEP CRAFTING ALL DAY LONG!

1 Create a world for you and your mates to play together!

2 Design your own custom skin.

3 Build an exact replica of your real-life house.

4 Craft enchanted diamond tools and armour ASAP! You're most likely to find diamonds between Y levels 5-12, so get digging!

5 Tame a Wolf to help you fend off mobs at night.

6 Open doors when building underwater to create an air pocket so you can breathe!

7 Decorate your world with epic pixel art statues!

8 Make a compass and a map for exploring.

9 Protect the Villagers — trading with them can help you in a jam!

10 Enchant a pickaxe with Silk Touch to mine full blocks without breaking them.

11 Stash your most valuable items in an Ender chest.

12 Don't forget to surround your base with light to keep away nasty mobs!

13
Build a small base around your portal in The Nether so your way home doesn't get destroyed!

14
Sneak to place items on utility blocks like furnaces and looms.

15
You can craft cool furniture designs using the set block command and half a bed.

16
Watch YouTube! It's full of crafting inspo!

17
Make elevators to quickly climb your base using soul sand and water!

18
Try raiding a Desert Temple or Woodland Mansion for top level loot!

BE A MINECRAFT MASTER!

19
Organise your hotbar so that you can switch between items quickly.

20
Label your storage chests with signs. Double up signs and frames for a cool hack!

21
Take pen to paper to sketch out new ideas and build plans.

22
Make a sweet triple-monitor gaming set up using banners!

23
Quickly explore caves by using a composter, lever and piston to get X-ray vision!

24
Defeat the Ender Dragon!

76 WAYS TO BOSS THE BLOCKS!

25

Help keep your base safe from Creepers by taming Ocelots!

26
ALWAYS take a water bucket to The Nether!

27
Use farms to make gathering resources easier.

28
Don't waste gold crafting tools or armour – save it for golden food.

29
Use golden apples to cure Zombie Villagers to get the best trade deals!

30
Take snowballs with you if you're going to be battling Blazes.

31

Upgrade your portal game! Experiment with different designs to make your portal the coolest ever!

32
Instead of crafting new tools, use an anvil to repair them.

33
Don't forget to build a beacon so you can always find your base.

34
Use trapdoors to crawl into tiny spaces you wouldn't normally fit in.

35
When cooking big batches of food, use a lava bucket instead of coal in the furnace.

36
Some ores spawn more frequently in specific biomes or between certain Y levels, so keep this in mind if you're looking for something in particular.

37
Push glass blocks down over objects using a piston to make cool displays.

38
Test out different seeds in Creative Mode to find the perfect world before you start a new Survival Mode adventure.

39
Instead of using a lava pit to destroy items, make a trapdoor bin — it's safer!

40
Always place torches on the same side when mining so you can easily find your way back.

41
Put out the flames of campfires with a shovel for a cool shelf design.

42
Fight Creepers with a flint and steel — they'll explode faster!

43
Design your own cool cape!

44
Use Nether portals to travel across the Overworld quickly.

45
Convert coal, redstone or lapis into blocks so you can carry more while you're mining.

46
Wear a pumpkin head when collecting Ender pearls to make Endermen easier to handle.

47
Unleash your inner Spider-Man with honey blocks to walk on walls!

48
Use the Fortunate III enchantment when you're mining for diamonds.

49
Stock up on bones to make bone meal. It'll help crops like wheat grow faster.

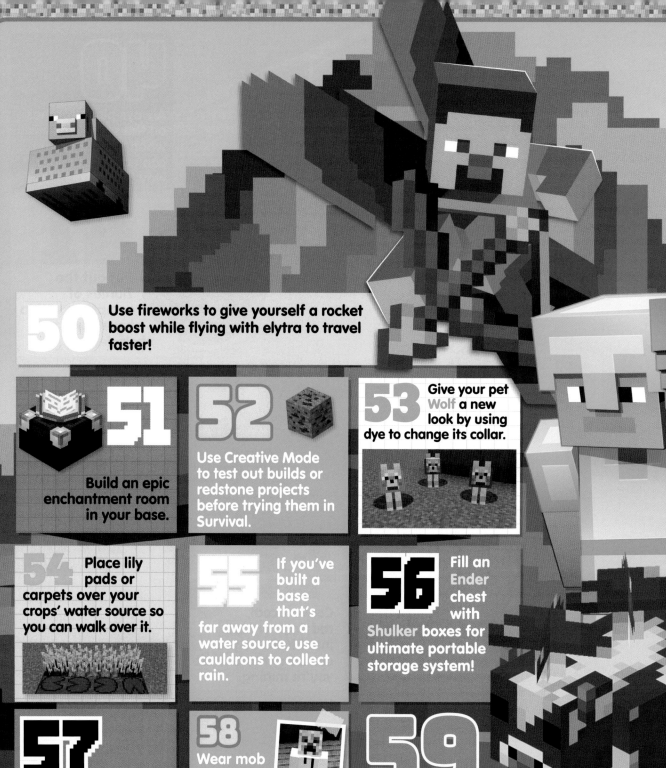

50 Use fireworks to give yourself a rocket boost while flying with elytra to travel faster!

51 Build an epic enchantment room in your base.

52 Use Creative Mode to test out builds or redstone projects before trying them in Survival.

53 Give your pet Wolf a new look by using dye to change its collar.

54 Place lily pads or carpets over your crops' water source so you can walk over it.

55 If you've built a base that's far away from a water source, use cauldrons to collect rain.

56 Fill an Ender chest with Shulker boxes for ultimate portable storage system!

57 If you're swarmed by mobs, empty a water bucket to buy yourself some time!

58 Wear mob heads to blend in and sneak past mobs — they reduce the range of detection!

59 Make a Mooshroom pen for a super-efficient food source.

60 Use a minecart and a lectern to create a working desk that you can actually read and write at!

61 Create a colour-changing rainbow Sheep by naming it jeb_ with a nametag!

62 Deflect Skeleton arrows with your shield – if you hit another mob, they'll start fighting with the Skeleton and leave you alone!

63

Place doors at least one block above ground to stop Zombies breaking in!

64

Decorate your base with a cake — it's the perfect easy-access snack!

65

Make a working basketball hoop using a cobweb and signs!

66

Stock up on Ghast tears every time you visit The Nether.

67

Build stylish animal pens without using fences by using honey floors instead.

68

Craft a secret room by sneak placing a painting on sign ends — you'll be able to walk right through it!

69

Experiment with different blocks to make sick statues.

70

Arm yourself with a shield as well as a sword!

71

If you have multiple beacons, change the colours with stained glass to tell them apart.

72

Place beds on top of armour stands wearing iron helmets to make a cool sofa!

73

Keep an eye on your Wolf's tail — the lower the tail, the lower the health!

74

Stack chests to save space by pressing sneak while placing them.

75

Craft an Iron Golem to help protect your base or a village.

BUILD AN AWESOME ARMOUR EQUIPPER!

YOU'LL NEED:

 8 REDSTONE

 2 REDSTONE REPEATERS

 8 DISPENSERS

 5 STONE SLABS

 1 BLOCK OF IRON

 1 PRESSURE PLATE

1 Dig out an L-shaped trench that's two blocks wide and three blocks long. Next place a dispenser and redstone inside the trench. Pop a pressure plate on top of the dispenser.

2 Surround the pressure plate with dispensers so that there's two on either side and one on top. Make sure the one on top is facing down.

3 Place two slabs at the back of both sides of the dispensers. Add redstone repeaters to the back two slabs and then place redstone on top of each front slab as well as on the ground between them.

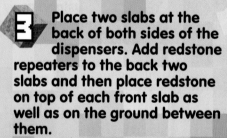

4 Add another slab to the top half of the top dispenser at the back and place redstone on both.

5 Fill the dispensers with armour, weapons and splash potions.

YOU CAN'T GET HIPPER THAN AN ARMOUR EQUIPPER!

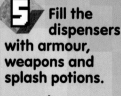

WHEN YOU STAND ON THE PRESSURE PLATE, IT'LL AUTOMATICALLY EQUIP YOU WITH ARMOUR! PERFECT IF YOU NEED TO GET BATTLE READY IN A HURRY!

MINECRAFT™

MAKEOVER MASTER!

USE THIS GRID TO DRAW YOURSELF AS A MINECRAFT CHARACTER!

Why not design a brand-new mob, too? You could give your pet a makeover, Minecraft-style or design the creature you always wanted as a pet IRL – like a shark-icorn or dino-dog!

MARVEL MULTIVERSE

AVENGERS TOWER

Forget about a helipad, this terrific tower has an elytra pad! Build a water elevator to take you to the top of the tower in style and make sure you've got a bow and plenty of arrows on hand just in case you need to take to the skies like Hawkeye!

BUILD TIP!

When tackling a big building, start with the corners or outer frame first, then go back and fill in the rest!

OOPS... WRONG PORTAL!

YOUR FRIENDLY NEIGHBOURHOOD SPIDER-MINE!

Prefer a more chilled out build? Create a cool office space to stash your loot!

DAILY BUGLE

Read all about it! Marvel's Daily Bugle might be the best place for Spidey gossip, but why not make yours the best place for Spiders?! Grab a Spider spawner from an abandoned mineshaft and make your own Spider farm – perfect for harvesting XP!

Use a mix of blocks, stairs and walls to create texture in your builds. This will make them look more realistic!

SANCTUM SANCTORUM

Chanel your inner Doctor Strange and create a magical hideout filled with all your fave potions, crafting goodies and enchanting tables! Plus, you can even create a special room with Nether and End portals so you can visit different dimensions, just like our fave sorcerer!

SUPERHERO SKINS!

IRON MAN

I'M COOL X3000!

★ If you're the joker of your Minecraft crew then you need the skin to prove it! Try using this in Creative to fly around and get the full Iron Man experience.

CAPTAIN AMERICA

★ You can't beat the old red, white and blue of Captain America's epic outfit!

BLACK PANTHER

★ No one will mess with you if you rock around the map as T'Challa - anyone who does will probably end up regretting it. Wakanda forever!

GO TEAM A!

THOR

★ We saw that Thor loved Fortnite in Avengers: Endgame, so why not Minecraft?! Run around as the Lord of Thunder, leaving everyone in awe of your cape.

SCARLET WITCH

★ The Scarlet Witch's skin might not include universe-bending powers, but it does come with a cool outfit!

THE HULK

★ This Hulk might be the same size as everyone else, but he looks just as strong and ready to SMASH any Creeper he sees!

CREEPER OR VEG?

Creepers are lean, green, mean machines – and vegetables aren't!
Can you tell a Creeper from a vegetable?

A.

CREEPER OR VEGETABLE?

B.

CREEPER OR VEGETABLE?

C.

CREEPER OR VEGETABLE?

D.

CREEPER OR VEGETABLE?

E.

CREEPER OR VEGETABLE?

F.

CREEPER OR VEGETABLE?

HISSSS!

ANSWERS
A. Creeper B. Vegetable C. Vegetable D. Creeper E. Vegetable F. Creeper

47

BE A HARDCORE HERO!

SURVIVE MINECRAFT'S TOUGHEST MODE WITH OUR HARDCORE HACKS!

SKY HIGH!

Want a mob-proof place to chill safely in at night? Then you need a floating sky base! You can even use waterfalls as a quick and easy way to get in and out – win!

PACK A BED!

ALWAYS make sure you've got access to a bed so you can snooze in peace and keep those pesky Phantoms at bay!

SNACK ATTACK!

🪓 Make sure you're always topping up your hunger bar and have plenty of snacks packed. There's nothing worse than getting caught snacking mid-fight or having to run away, depleting your bar even more!

TOP TIP: NEVER dig straight down!

STORE MORE!

🪓 There are loads of great ways to make your pockets a little deeper in Minecraft! Use Donkeys, Llamas and Mules to boost your storage on the go, and don't forget about shulker boxes, Ender chests and bundles, too!

MATERIALS MATTER!

🪓 Stock up on plenty of wood as quickly as you can! Torches, a basic shelter and some simple weapons are the key to getting through the first night. It'll take time to build up better resources, but once you do, you can start tackling the trickier areas, like Woodland Mansions!

TOP TIP:

Woodland Mansions are full of Evokers and Vexes, so make sure you've got enchanted diamond armour and a sword before you go in!

VILLAGER HACKS!

GET THE MOST OUT OF THE LOCALS!

RAID IT!

It's always worth checking what loot you can pinch from the houses whenever you come across a new village!

VILLAGER HOTEL!

Build a safe space for your Villagers to live and give them all their own room, bed and job. That way, if you ever need to buy anything, you know exactly where to go!

GOLEM GAINS!

If you want an endless supply of iron without having to mine, trap a Zombie in the sky above a village and build a sneaky underwater lava pit. The Villagers will start making Iron Golems, who'll then fall into the lava!

WILL YOU SURVIVE A NIGHT IN MINECRAFT?

CHOOSE WISELY OR FACE THE ZOMBIES!

START!

You're stranded, first priority is...

BUILDING A SHELTER →

You need to get resources! Which do you mine first...

STARTING A FIRE FOR WARMTH

UNDERGROUND FOR STONES AND METAL

TREES FOR WOOD

GAME OVER!
You've attracted too much Skeleton attention.

What's most important...

FARMING ANIMALS

FARMING CROPS

You decide to fight! What do you do...

SHOOT FROM A DISTANCE

SET TRAPS

You're getting pretty hungry. You...

COOK UP SOME GRUB

QUICK SNACK SOME FRUIT

GAME OVER!
You took too long and Creepers found you!

I WILL SURVIVE!

YOU SURVIVED!
It's not ALL about crafting, and you have what it takes! You can face anything.

SPOT THE DIFFERENCE!

UH OH! SOMETHING WEIRD'S GOING ON HERE! CAN YOU SPOT THE FIVE DIFFERENCES IN THE PICTURES BELOW?

HOW DO PIGS WRITE SECRET MESSAGES?

WITH INVISIBLE OINK!

ANSWER:

THE MINECRAFT

EXPLORER'S GUIDE

ARE YOU A TRUE MINECRAFT ADVENTURER?

PINK SHEEP

Although you can dye them whatever colour you like, it's very rare to come across a naturally pink Sheep in the wild.

GIANT MUSHROOM ISLAND

It takes a real *fungi* to track down these islands!

TUNDRA LAVA LAKE

NEED SOMETHING TO WARM YOU UP ON YOUR POLAR EXPLORATION? SAY NO MORE!

THERE'S ALWAYS MORE TO EXPLORE!

UNDERGROUND FOSSIL

The bones of huge ancient creatures are buried under the desert sands just waiti to be discovered.

ICE SPIKES BIOME

THIS FROSTY BIOME IS FULL OF HUGE ICE STRUCTURES THAT CAN REACH HEIGHTS OF OVER 50 BLOCKS!

DESERT TEMPLE

Raid these sandy structures for loads of epic treasure!

FLOATING ISLANDS

These glitched out islands in the sky can sometimes be randomly generated in new worlds.

WITCH COVEN

One **Witch** is tough enough! Make sure you're prepared before you take on a whole group of them.

REDWOOD FOREST

Also known as Mega Taiga, these super-rare biomes are full of massive spruce trees and mushrooms.

JUNGLE TEMPLE

Dangerous foes and rare items are hidden deep within these mysterious temples.

POWER PROFILE!

DAMAGE ALERT!

Don't get on their bad side! If you deal damage to an untamed Wolf, it activates its Angry Mode — their eyes turn red, they growl and, worst of all, they attack you!

WOLF

DID YOU KNOW?

★ When Wolves are tamed, they gain a red collar and you can even make them sit and stay, just like a pet pup!

★ Tamed Wolves can teleport! If their owner moves more than 12 blocks away, they can teleport back to them.

★ They beg for food! Hold meat or a bone in front of them and they'll tilt their head as if to say 'please feed me'.

★ You can tell how healthy a Wolf is by its tail — the lower the tail, the lower the health!

★ Feeding a Wolf pup meat can help it grow up a little bit faster.

POWER UP!

Wolves can be tamed! Just give a dog a bone and you'll have a loyal companion who'll follow you and even fight for you when nasty mobs show up.

STATS:

STRENGTH	
SPEED	
AGILITY	
SKILL	
COOLNESS	

OVERALL >>>> 7

COMICCRAFT

DAVE
MAX
MINNIE & CRAFTY

GET READY FOR SOME MINI MINECRAFT LOLS WITH MAX, DAVE, CRAFTY AND MINNIE!

BLOCKED!

Hey! Can I borrow your new diamond sw

BLOCKED!

You can't block people in person! What are you going to do, box yourself in?

That's GENIUS!

Ah, peace at last...

CUBE CAR!

I've built a sweet new ride, but there's just one problem...

I'm a master builder. Maybe I can help!

Someone stole my woolly cool wheels!

Woollen wheels? With Minnie around? There's no helping him...

SKELETON SNICKERS!

Right this way, sir.

Are you ready to order, sir?

Hmm ...

I'll have the spare ribs!

55

TOP 11
MINECRAFT
MASH-UPS!

11 LITTLEBIGPLANET!

Exclusive to PlayStation editions, this awesome pack lets you explore a massive new world. You can even change your skin to look like Sackboy!

10

POWER RANGERS!

This mighty morphin' Minecraft mash-up features all your fave Power Rangers. The only problem is deciding which one you want to be!

9 THE SIMPSONS!

You can transform yourself into one of The Simpsons with this super-fun skin pack. Baby Maggie looks so funny!

8

MAGIC: THE GATHERING!

Even if you've never heard of the Magic games before, this mash-up has loads of cool looking new skins to customise your character!

7

STAR WARS!

Bring balance to the Force with these amazing Star Wars style skins, from a blocky galaxy far, far away!

6

MINECRAFT STORY MODE!

We loved playing Minecraft Story Mode, so getting to play as Jesse in regular Minecraft is just so awesome!

MINECRAFT MASH-UPS!

5

HALLOWEEN!

Fancy something spooky? Then this is the pack for you! Make it Halloween all year round with **Dracula** and **Frankenstein** in this creepy mash-up pack!

> WHO DID FRANKENSTEIN TAKE TO THE DANCE?

> HIS GHOUL FRIEND!

> WHAT DO YOU CALL THE DOCTOR IN MINECRAFT?

> BLOCK-TER WHO!

POLICE PUBLIC CALL BOX

4

DOCTOR WHO!

Whether you're a **Doctor** or a **Dalek** these sweet skins are perfect for adventuring through space and time — and Minecraft!

SUPER MARIO!

Mario mixed with Minecraft? Yes please! With loads of cool character skins and an incredible map, this mash-up is insane!

2

MARVEL HEROES!

Avengers assemble! Boss Minecraft like your fave hero with these super skins, including Spidey, Captain America and Hulk!

1

ADVENTURE TIME!

This classic Minecraft mash-up is totally mathematical! Explore The Land of Ooo as best bros Jake and Finn. You can even visit The Treehouse or The Candy Kingdom!

BUILD A DINOSAUR DEN!

TAKE YOUR MINECRAFT WORLD TO THE JURASSIC ERA WITH THIS EPIC DINO DEN!

Unwelcome Warning!

● Let intruders know that your base is off limits! If a scary sign and guard dog doesn't make them turn and run, decorate the walls with creepy mob trophies!

TOP TIP!

Use green stained glass to make windows. They'll look like part of the T-Rex's pattern and let light inside your base.

Secret Entrance!

● When building your T-Rex's legs, make sure they're hollow so that you can climb inside. If you want to hide your entrance, use vines – they'll blend right in!

Mega Mouth!

● Your dinosaur's mouth is the perfect place for a lookout! Load it up with chests filled with bows and arrows and snowballs to keep enemies at bay. Plus, your T-Rex's jaggy teeth are just like battlements that you can hide behind!

Scare Necessities!

● Your base might look scary on the outside, but it still needs to feel like home on the inside. Make a bedroom, armoury and kitchen so you have everything you need.

LET'S COLOUR!

ADD A SPLASH OF COLOUR TO BRING STEVE TO LIFE!

TALK ABOUT COLOUR BLOCKING!

HOW TO CRAFT A REDSTONE BLOCK

Do you need a cool night light to help you read this epic book in bed? Why not craft yourself this awesome redstone block!

ASK AN ADULT TO HELP!

YOU WILL NEED:
- An empty tissue box
- Glowsticks — small enough to fit in the tissue box
- Red cellophane
- Scissors
- Sticky tape
- Masking tape
- Grey paint

STEP 1
Cover the tissue box in masking tape and draw the redstone pattern on all sides.

STEP 2
Ask an adult to carefully cut out the shapes you have drawn. Now paint the box grey and leave to dry. You may need two coats.

STEP 3
Stick squares of red cellophane inside the box covering the holes.

STEP 4
Put the glowstick inside and see it glow! EPIC!

MINECRAFT DUNGEONS

EVERYTHING YOU NEED TO KNOW ABOUT THIS CRAFTY DUNGEON CRAWLER!

WHOLE NEW GAME!

Although Dungeons is set in the Minecraft world we all know and love, it's a totally new gaming experience! Based on retro dungeon-crawlers, you'll see all the action unfold from above, which helps to give the Minecraft world a fresh new look and feel!

COOL COMBAT!

One of the coolest things about Dungeons has to be the combat gameplay! Not only can you switch between close-up melee action and long distance ranged attacks, but you can also power up loads of epic weapons and enchantments to unleash special attacks!

EPIC QUEST!

Prepare to go on the most epic Minecraft adventure yet! There are loads of cool levels and locations to explore and battle your way through, as you go on a quest to stop the evil Arch-Illager mob. You can even tag in your mates to help you, in local and online Co-op Modes.

WHO'S NEW?!

MEET SOME OF THE NEW MOBS WHO'LL BE POPPING UP IN MINECRAFT DUNGEONS!

NAMELESS ONE

KEY GOLEM

REDSTONE MONSTROSITY

ARCH-ILLAGER

NEW STUFF!

There are plenty of familiar faces to be found in Dungeons, but there's also loads of new stuff to discover if you've never played it before! Get to grips with wicked new mobs — like the Skeleton Vanguard — as you explore eerie new locations, such as the Creeper Woods and the Fiery Forge!

MINECRAFT DUNGEONS

ULTIMATE DLC
EVERY AWESOME EXTRA – RATED!

JUNGLE AWAKENS

Welcome to the jungle! With three missions to battle through, this wild DLC is packed full of new features, including awesome variants of fave foes such as Mossy Skeletons and Jungle Zombies. Plus, there are two new terrors to take on, the Leapleaf and the Whisperer, as well as an epic boss battle with the Jungle Abomination!

OUR RATING: 6/10

CREEPING WINTER

This super-cool DLC takes you on a chilling adventure to face the ultimate wintery baddie, the Wretched Wraith! As well as amazing, icy environments to explore, you'll also get a bunch of other awesome extras including two new skins, an Arctic Fox pet, the Winter's Touch bow and the Ice Wand artifact.

OUR RATING: 6/10

HOWLING PEAKS

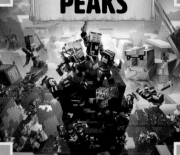

Reach brand-new heights in Minecraft Dungeons as a strange power corrupts the mountains and threatens to take over the world! With new mobs to take on, like the Squall Golem and Mountaineer, as well as 16 new items, three missions and three cosmetics, Howling Peaks will have you gaming for ages!

OUR RATING: 7 /10

FLAMES OF THE NETHER

This DLC turns up the heat as you head into the heart of the fiery Nether! With more new missions than any other DLC pack, there are six new locations to explore, from the creepy Nether Wastes to the secret Soul Sand Valley. But if all that sounds too spooky, don't worry! You'll also get an adorable new pet – a Baby Ghast!

OUR RATING: 8/10

HIDDEN DEPTHS

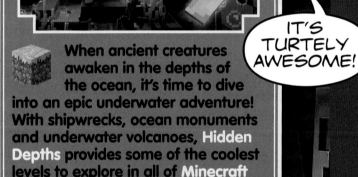

IT'S TURTELY AWESOME!

When ancient creatures awaken in the depths of the ocean, it's time to dive into an epic underwater adventure! With shipwrecks, ocean monuments and underwater volcanoes, Hidden Depths provides some of the coolest levels to explore in all of Minecraft Dungeons!

OUR RATING: 8/10

ECHOING VOID

Explore The End in this epic DLC! Packed with loads of awesome Ender mobs, including SEVEN different Endersent variants, Blastlings and your very own Endermite pet. If all that wasn't enough, you also get a whopping 20 new items – more than any other DLC!

OUR RATING: 9/10

WHO WILL WIN?
CREEPERS V

BIG GREEN BADDIES! CREEPERS

☑ SCARY FACE!

☑ SNEAKY CAMO!

☑ CHARGED UP!

☒ EXPLOSIVE!

SKELETONS

☑ **AWESOME RIDES!**

☑ **BOWS AND ARROWS!**

☑ **GREAT AIM!**

☒ **FRAGILE BODIES!**

BAD BONY BOWMEN! SKELETONS

WINNER! SKELETONS

Keeping the Creepers at a distance with their bows, an exploding Creeper is no match for Minecraft's Skeletons!

EPIC CRAFTER

HOW MANY OF THESE TASKS CAN YOU DO?

RECREATE YOUR OWN BEDROOM IN CREATIVE MODE! ⬜

CREATE A CREEPER FARM! ⬜

BUILD A GIANT SKY BRIDGE BETWEEN AS MANY BIOMES AS YOU CAN! ⬜

MAKE YOUR OWN MINIGAME! ⬜

GATHER ALL THE MATERIALS YOU NEED TO BUILD A BASE WHILE WALKING BACKWARDS! ⬜

WE OBVS USE SUN-*BLOCK* ON OUR *SKINS!*

BUILD AN EPIC TREEHOUSE! ⬜

CHALLENGES!

MAKE A REDSTONE CONTRAPTION – THAT ACTUALLY WORKS!

CREATE A CUSTOM SKIN!

GO ON A NETHER ADVENTURE!

SURVIVE THE NIGHT IN HARDCODE MODE WITH NO SHELTER AND NO SWORDS!

TIME YOURSELF BUILDING A BASIC SHELTER THEN SEE IF YOU CAN BEAT YOUR OWN TIME!

TAME EVERY MOB!

BUILD A WATERSLIDE!

DEFEAT THE ENDER DRAGON USING ONLY SNOWBALLS!

71

PIXEL ARTWORK!

THESE TIPS WILL HELP YOU BUILD A MINECRAFT MASTERPIECE!

STEP 1

● Search online for a cool template. It's a good idea to practise with simple designs first before building anything too complicated!

FROM THE MUSHROOM KINGDOM TO MINECRAFT!

STEP 2

● Create a new flat world in Creative Mode with no structures. Remember to set your difficulty to Peaceful or a rogue Creeper might wreck your hard work!

LET'S GET THIS ARTY PARTY STARTED!

STEP 3

● Pick out the colours you'll need to build your design from the Creative menu. Don't be afraid to experiment with different blocks!

STEP 4

● Start from the bottom of your design and work your way up, line by line. For more complex art, it's a good idea to build your outline first and then colour in.

STEP 5

● Once you've mastered the basics, use graph paper to plan out your own designs. Stand back and admire your masterpiece!

Check out these other designs!

POWER PROFILE!

DAMAGE ALERT!

If a Bee successfully attacks a player and poisons them, it loses its stinger and can't attack anymore. Stingerless Bees don't survive for long after the initial attack.

BEE

POWER UP!

Just like IRL, Minecraft Bees are pollinators. This means they can transfer pollen from flowers or berry bushes to your farm, helping your crops to grow!

DID YOU KNOW?

⭐ If one Bee is attacked, every nearby Bee also gets angry, swarming and attacking the culprit!

⭐ Bees calm down quickly if their attack isn't successful. After 25 seconds they'll be back to neutral.

⭐ If you're holding a flower, Bees will follow you, and if you give them a flower, they'll start breeding!

⭐ After Bees have finished pollinating, they return to their hives to make honey. You can tell if honey is ready to collect when the hive starts dripping.

⭐ Bees live in colonies and each nest can house up to three Bees in it.

STATS:

STRENGTH	
SPEED	
AGILITY	
SKILL	
COOLNESS	

OVERALL ›››6.5

COMICCRAFT

DAVE

MAX

MINNIE & CRAFTY

GET READY FOR SOME MINI MINECRAFT LOLS WITH MAX, DAVE, CRAFTY AND MINNIE!

CAT-ASTROPHE!

MEOW!

Look, Minnie got trapped trying to catch birds!

Don't worry, I'll save her!

Here Kitty...

EEK!

CRACK!

Well, you got her down, at least.

CASTLE CALAMITY!

I'm going to build an epic castle!

300 HOURS LATER...

Finally finished. I can't wait to move in!

THAT NIGHT...

KNOCK! KNOCK!

Who could that be?

Surprise!

I brought you a housewarming gift!

It's a potted cactus!

BUT —

HISSSS!

Erm, I don't think that's a cactus, Max...

BOOM!

Back to square one then?

75

MYSTERY

QUEST 1

CHART A COURSE!

Find map-making materials and other useful items!

PAPER ☐   HELMET ☐

COMPASS ☐   BOOTS ☐

APPLE ☐   FEATHER ☐

LET'S MAKE A MAP!

X	B	J	H	C	K	C	B
X	O	F	E	O	P	F	H
O	O	E	L	M	I	L	Z
P	T	A	M	P	E	F	U
A	S	T	E	A	L	Z	W
P	D	H	T	S	E	E	B
E	H	E	Q	S	W	X	V
R	A	R	A	P	P	L	E

QUEST 2

JUST ORCHID-ING!

Find your way through the maze to the blue orchid so you can make dye!

START

FINISH

QUEST!

WORK YOUR WAY THROUGH THESE QUESTS TO CRAFT AN AWESOME MYSTERY ITEM!

I'M THE CRAFTING KING!

QUEST 3

SLAY THE CREEPER!

We need gunpowder from a Creeper. Find your sword among all these other tools!

CRAFTING TIME!

Put your light blue dye, feather, and gunpowder together. Unscramble these letters to find out what you've made!

I	R	R	E	K	F	O	W		O	C	K	E	R	T

F			↓		O							↓		E

CAN YOU COMPLETE THE QUEST?

77

SHIPWRECK!

Arrgh, mateys! Dive into an aquatic adventure with this pirate shipwreck!

Head On!

● Ancient ships used to have creepy carved heads on the front to scare off evil spirits. Our pirate ship has an eerie Ender Dragon head at the front, so enemies better watch out!

DIVE IN!

Lookout!

● When you're sailing the seven seas, you need to be able to spot any dangers from miles away. By building a lookout called a crow's nest, you'll always be able to see what's coming!

Hidden Treasure!

● If there's one thing that pirates love, it's treasure! Underwater caves are a perfect place to stash your valuable items.

Secret Cabin!

● Underwater hideouts are the best! They're super-secret and you won't meet as many nasty mobs under the sea. A sunken ship's cabin gives you the perfect hiding place and a dry place to sleep!

WHO'S HIDING?

OH NO, STEVE'S LOST IN A SEA OF ZOMBIES! CAN YOU FIND HIM AND THE OTHER LOST MOBS?

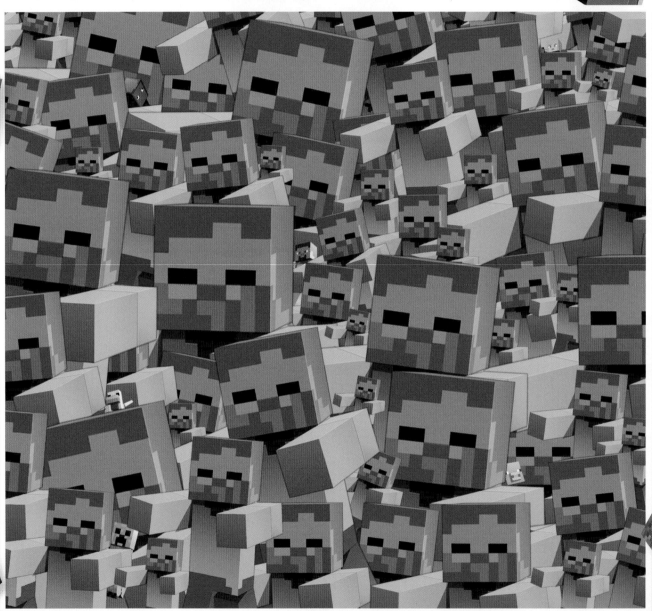

WHO'S HIDING?

STEVE   PIG   SQUID

CHICKEN   CREEPER   ALEX

ANSWER

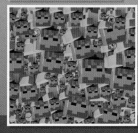

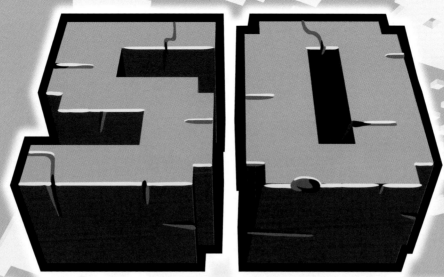

50 BLOCK-BUSTING MINECRAFT TIPS

DON'T BE A BLOCKHEAD!
BECOME THE SHARPEST PICKAXE
IN THE ENDER CHEST
WITH OUR BLOCK-BUSTING TIPS!

50 BLOCK-BUSTING MINECRAFT TIPS

1. **Zombie**-proof doors by placing the door one block above the ground. **Zombies** can't jump and attack doors at the same time.

2. Dig on layer 12 on the y axis to find diamonds quicker!

3. Destroy all the wood in a tree to make floating leaves disappear.

4. Visit the **End City** to find purpur blocks!

5. Most blocks ignore the rules of gravity and can float in the air!

6. Sand and gravel will fall if they're not supported. So don't dig beneath them!

7. If gravel or sand falls on your head you can suffocate!

8. You need four Prismarine Shards to make one block of Prismarine!

9. Don't get lost in **The Nether**! Moving eight blocks in **The Nether** is equal to one block in the ~~Overworld~~!

10. You can trap mobs in glass blocks using a piston!

11. Destroying a bush will bag you two sticks!

12. You can collect cobwebs by using shears on them!

13. Mine for redstone ore veins at the bottom 16 layers on your map!

14. The End Portal can't be destroyed or mined!

15. Find an **End Ship** to get an **Ender Dragon** head!

16 It takes four minutes ten seconds to break obsidian with your fist, so use a diamond pickaxe instead!

17 If you place water or lava a block above a cactus it'll break!

18 If you need crops, steal them from villages! Beetroot, carrots, potatoes and wheat all spawn there!

19 Build your base on a Mooshroom Island. Hostile mobs can't spawn there!

20 Netherrack was originally called Bloodstone! Creepy!

21 Mob spawner blocks cannot be crafted, mined or placed!

22 Even the air in Minecraft is made with blocks — air blocks!

23 Ditch the Cat! If it's sitting on your chest you won't be able to open it!

24 Cats don't take fall damage — neither do Ocelots! So don't chase them off cliffs!

25 Fully charge your bow so it does more damage than a diamond sword!

26 Sea lanterns only spawn in ocean monuments!

Gold Hoe

27 Golden hoes are useless, don't waste your gold crafting them!

28 Cover your base in slabs as mobs can't spawn on them!

29 Don't use soul sand around your base! If a Skeleton or Zombie stands on it during the day they won't catch fire!

30 If you place ice blocks under soul sand, players are slowed down!

31 Mobs can't sprint! Make a completely mob-proof door by placing a pressure plate far enough away from the door so that you can sprint in!

32 Place a pressure plate on the inside of a door and it'll close itself behind you!

33 Don't throw stuff at The Wither. It's immune to all projectiles!

34 Save wood by crafting one wooden pickaxe and using it to get stone to craft other tools!

35 Block Skeleton arrows with your sword so you don't take damage!

36 Only break Ender chests with a silk touch pickaxe or you will lose the chest and the loot inside!

37 Build your base underground so you can mine at night!

38 Throw dirt and gravel away. Don't store them, it's a waste of space and you'll never use it!

39 Don't leave your Snow Golems in the rain, they'll die!

40 Hide the entrance to your underground base under a tree. No one will suspect it's there!

50 BLOCK-BUSTING MINECRAFT TIPS

41 Run away from large hordes of enemies or you'll get overwhelmed!

42 If you mine stone with a silk touch pickaxe, you'll get stone, not cobblestone!

43 The only mob that spawns in the Deep Dark is the Warden!

44 Light up underground tunnels in the day so mobs won't spawn there overnight!

45 Chorus trees are grown from chorus flowers which you can find in The End!

46 Carry water buckets when you're mining for diamonds, they often spawn next to lava!

47 Take a bed with you in your inventory so you can sleep in a makeshift shelter.

48 You can dry a wet sponge block in a furnace then use it to absorb water again!

49 Don't try to kill a Skeleton if you've just newly spawned in hardcore mode. You won't win!

50 Build a moat to keep the Endermen away!

LAVA LAIR!

THIS EPIC BUILD IS TOO HOT TO HANDLE!

TRAP DOOR!

● Place a pressure plate on the ground and surround it with doors. Make sure the door handles are pointing away from the plate. When a mob steps on it, the doors will swing shut and they'll be stuck!

THIS LAVA WILL BE THE ENDER ME!

SNEAKY BLOCKS!

● We've used magma blocks for the floor so that any intruders who walk over this will take fire damage. Don't worry though, if you sneak over these blocks, you won't take any damage yourself!

FLAME TIPPED TOWERS!

PARKOUR PRO!

● The only way on and off this lava island is a petrifying parkour path! If anyone wants to get to your lair, they'll need to show off some top skills... or else!

I LAVA GOOD LAIR!

MAZE MAYHEM!

HELP STEVE GET TO THE BOTTOM OF THIS MAZE AND FIND THE DIAMONDS!

START!

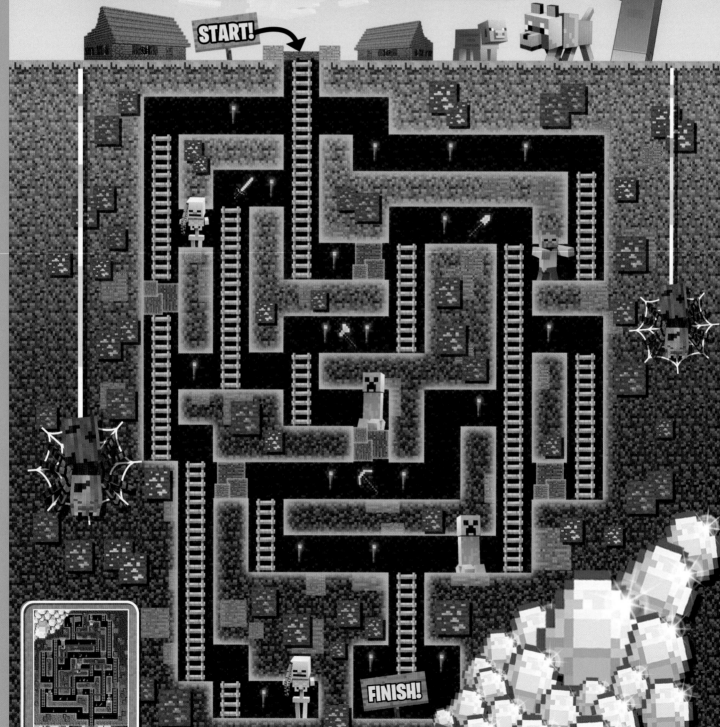

FINISH!

ANSWER:

88

MAKE A MINECRAFT TORCH!

YOU WILL NEED:

CARDBOARD • **STICKY TAPE** • **BROWN PAPER** • **SCISSORS** • **BATTERY TEA LIGHT**

1 ● Ask an adult to cut a rectangle from cardboard 20cm by 25cm.

25cm
20cm

2 ● Ask an adult to score four lines an equal distance apart on the cardboard using scissors.

3 ● Bend the cardboard into a rectangle and use tape to hold it together.

4 ● Cut a square out of cardboard and tape it to the bottom of the tube.

5 ● Cut the brown paper to cover the tube leaving 4cm above the top.

6 ● Decorate the paper to look like a Minecraft torch and tape round the tube.

7 ● Pop the tea light in the top and your torch is ready to glow!

2 LOCATION IS EVERYTHING!

Flip a coin to see where you'll be creating your masterpiece.

HEADS = THE OVERWORLD   **TAILS =** THE NETHER

3 WHAT'LL IT BE?!

Roll the dice (or get a family member to pick a number from 1-6) to find out what you'll be building!

A GIANT SELF-PORTRAIT	A HEARTY PIRATE SHIP
AN UNDERGROUND LAIR	THE TALLEST SKYSCRAPER
A TERRIFYING ROLLERCOASTER	THE COOLEST CASTLE EVER

4 A HELPING HAND!

Look around you... IRL! The number of people in the room with you right now are the amount of people you can draft in for help with your build!

5 DRAFT IT OUT!

Every good architect needs a plan! Draw your build before you get started and see how the real thing compares!

CHALLENGE YOURSELF TO BUILD SOMETHING NEW... UNLESS YOU'RE CHICKEN!

MOONCRAFT

JOIN US AS WE BOLDLY GO ON AN ADVENTURE TO THE MOON IN MINECRAFT!

SPACE STATION!
● Over in the distance you can spot the International Space Station. We used Minecraft banners instead of solar panels to make it look the part!

FLYING SAUCER!
● Looks like this spacecraft has caught a Creeper in its tractor beam! But is it beaming it up or down?

OLD SKOOL ROCKET!
● This bright red rocket is caught in orbit around our Minecraft moon. It looks pretty old though, how long has it been looping?

THE MOON!
● People say the moon is made out of cheese, but we made our Minecraft moon from white and grey wool. Perfect for a soft landing!

MOON FACT!
THE FIRST TIME MAN LANDED ON THE MOON WAS ON JULY 20, 1969!

SPACE SHUTTLE!

● In real life, we don't use the space shuttle to go to space any more, but it's such a cool space ship we had to build one of our own!

MOON LANDER!

● If you're going to land on the moon, you need a NASA moon lander! This one's on top of the moon, but it could have landed anywhere.

MOON FACT!
THE FIRST MOON LANDING WAS CALLED APOLLO 11 AND AMERICAN ASTRONAUTS NEIL ARMSTRONG AND BUZZ ALDRIN WERE THE FIRST MEN ON THE MOON!

POWER PROFILE!

DAMAGE ALERT!

If threatened, Llamas will attack players by spitting, but sometimes their spit will hit another Llama by mistake, and they'll start fighting among themselves!

LLAMA

DID YOU KNOW?

⭐ Llamas hate Wolves – they don't even need to be attacked to spit at them!

⭐ Unlike Horses, you can't add a saddle to a Llama so using a lead is the best way to move around together.

⭐ Although you can't ride them with a saddle, you can ride wild Llamas in order to tame them – but watch out, they might throw you off!

⭐ You can add brightly coloured carpets to your tamed Llama to make them the most fashionable mob in Minecraft!

⭐ Trader Llamas that have spawned naturally can't be tamed unless they've been unleashed first!

POWER UP!

Not only can you tame Llamas, they're also super-useful for carrying and transporting items!

STATS:

STRENGTH
SPEED
AGILITY
SKILL
COOLNESS

OVERALL >>> 5.5

COMICCRAFT

DAVE

MAX

MINNIE & CRAFTY

GET READY FOR SOME MINI MINECRAFT LOLS WITH MAX, DAVE, CRAFTY AND MINNIE!

CHEST DISTRESS!

Hi Dave! Got a Creeper situation outside. Can I use your chest to hold my sword?

HMM...

I'd rather I used my hands than my chest!

Ahem I meant that chest...

PAINT PRANK!

With our new gear, we're going to be able to take on anything! I'm gonna go and fight the Ender Dragon!

Have I seen Dave? You did WHAT?!

You replaced his diamonds with painted coal?!

Woof? Woof, woof... WOOF!

Well, that didn't go as planned.

Oops.

LAVA LOLS!

What should we play next? Parkour? Sky Wars? Prop Hunt?

Oh, I know! Help me find my lava bucket!

...Why do we never play The Floor is Lava at your house?

SPOT THE DIFFERENCE!

Can you spot all six differences between these two pictures?

CRAFT A CREEPER HEAD!

YOU WILL NEED:

CARDBOARD BOX · SCISSORS · PAINT BRUSH · PENCIL · TOOTHPICK · GREEN, BLACK AND WHITE PAINT

1

● Cut off the extra tabs on your box and sketch squares all over it – they don't have to be perfect!

2

DO THIS ACTIVITY UNDER THE SUPERVISION OF A PARENT OR GUARDIAN.

● Mix your colours and paint your box similar to a Creeper – use our guide here to help you!

3

● Use a toothpick to carefully poke eye-holes into the cardboard!

4 ● Now you have an awesome Creeper head!

BUILD A HAUNTED HOUSE!

ARE YOU BRAVE ENOUGH TO STEP INSIDE THIS MYSTERIOUS MINECRAFT MANSION?

DRAG ME OUTTA HERE!

MONSTER BEDROOM!

● Do you dare to cosy up in this cobweb-filled four poster bed? We don't think we could fall asleep underneath that wicked Wither painting without having nightmares!

DEADLY DUNGEON!

● This creepy cellar is full of Cave Spiders and super-scary monster spawners – no thanks! We hate to think what else might be lurking underneath a house this haunted...

ALARMING ATTIC!

● Packed full of bats, cobwebs and dusty old books, we really wouldn't be surprised if ghosts lived in this attic too!

PETRIFYING PARLOUR!

● Don't be fooled by the comfy sofas or the cosy fire – this is one chilling room! Take a close look and you'll discover haunted heads on the mantel and a scary suit of armour!

TOO SSSPOOKY FOR ME!

REBUILD IT!

USE THE GRID BELOW TO FIT THE BLOCKS BACK INTO YOUR MINECRAFT WORLD!

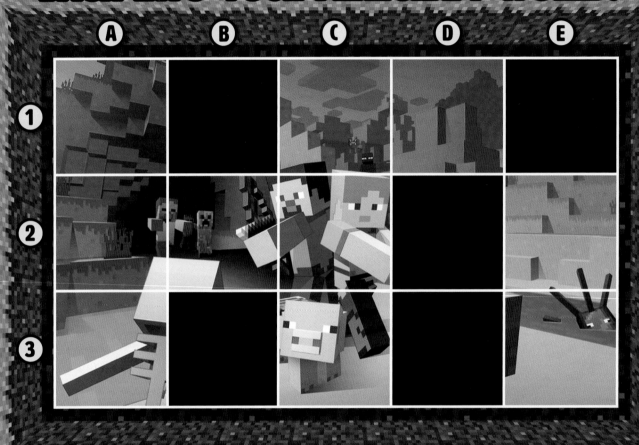

CODE ADVENTURE!

Uh-oh – Steve's Wolf is stuck in cobwebs!
Put the commands in the right order to help Steve free him!

KEY

UP
↑
← ↓ →
LEFT DOWN RIGHT

COMMAND BLOCKS

PICK UP
DIAMOND SWORD

MOVE RIGHT
THREE BLOCKS

FREE THE WOLF

MOVE RIGHT
THREE BLOCKS

MOVE RIGHT
ONE BLOCK

MOVE DOWN
TWO BLOCKS

SLAY THE ZOMBIE

MOVE UP
TWO BLOCKS

MOVE UP
FOUR BLOCKS

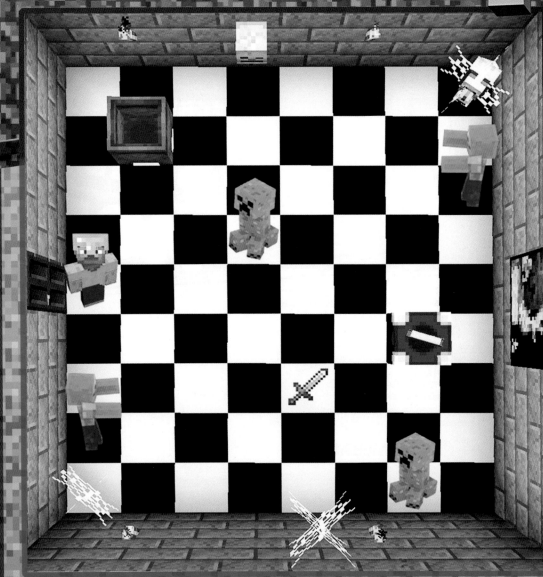

WRITE THE COMMANDS HERE!

1 Move right one block

2

3

4

5

6

7

8

9

SLIME

SECRETS!

SECRET 2

SLIMIEST MOBS!

SECRET 1

TYPES OF SLIME!

Minecraft has so many different types of slime it's hard to keep track!

SLIME
This mob comes in three sizes! Slimes don't die, they just split in two! Plus, tiny Slimes can't hurt you!

SLIMEBALL
Tiny Slimes drop these when killed. They can be used to craft leads, sticky pistons and more!

SLIME BLOCK
These blocks bounce you into the sky if you jump on them, like a snot-covered trampoline!

MAGMA CUBE
These Nether slimes come in three sizes and they all hurt!

MAGMA CREAM
Dropped by the larger Magma Cubes these are great for making potions of Fire Resistance.

It's time to rate these gross Minecraft mobs!

SLIME
You can't get slimier than a monster made of slime!

ZOMBIE
We reckon these undead uglies stink of slime!

SPIDER

Spiders aren't slimy but their webs are really super-gross!

CREEPER

They're not very slimy, but they do go boom!

SKELETON

They're spooky and scary, but they're dry as a bone!

MAGMA SLIME!

Get from Slime mob to magma block in five easy steps!

1 Harvest slimeballs by killing Slimes.

2 Gather blaze rods by defeating Blazes.

3 Craft blaze powder from the blaze rods.

4 Combine a slimeball with a blaze powder to make magma cream.

5 Use four magma creams to make a magma block!

103

TAKE THE LEAD!

Learn how to make and use leads in Minecraft from Slimes!

CRAFTING TIME!

INGREDIENTS

- STRING x 4
- SLIME x 1

RECIPE

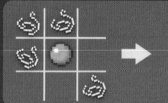

MOB RULES

1. Using the lead on a mob will tie it to one end, let you move it around or tie it in place.

2. Leads can only be used on passive mobs, except for Bats, Squid, Turtles and Villagers.

3. If you tie a mob to a fence, it will tend to stay within five blocks of the fence.

4. Tying a mob to a seven-block-tall fencepost will make it fly in the air!

5. A lead can stretch a total of ten blocks before breaking!

MY PET SLIME!

Learn why Slimes make the perfect pets!

NO TAMING!

Unlike other common Minecraft pets like Ocelots and Wolves, you don't have to tame a Slime! Once they spot you they will follow you, no matter what!

LADDER LOVE!

Did you know tiny Slimes can climb ladders? This makes Slimes excellent pets for when you've built an awesome treehouse base!

SLIME JOKES

We've got some jokes we bet you've never heard before!

HOW DO YOU FIND SLIMES?

SEARCH FOR THEM ON GOO-GLE!

WHAT DO YOU DO WITH BLUE SLIME?

CHEER IT UP!

WHAT'S A SLIME'S FAVOURITE GAME?

SLIME-ON SAYS!

TINY RISK!

Though big Slimes and small Slimes can hurt you, tiny Slimes don't do damage to players or mobs! Go fight some big Slimes and make some friends — literally!

MAKE A UNICORN PALACE

BUILD GOALS!

WATERSLIDE WONDER!

Make a splash with this epic rainbow waterslide! Hidden in the unicorn's tail, this secret water feature is loads of fun!

PONY PARTY!

Okay, so they might not be unicorns, but rainbow ponies are super-cute! Tame your faves and travel around your world in style!

RAINBOW READY!

Be ready for anything with this special rainbow lookout! Hidden high up in the clouds, it's the perfect place to keep watch and stash a secret chest full of goodies!

BEDROOM BLISS!

Cuddle up with your fave fluffy pet in this pink paradise! Use end rods to create sparkling bedside lava lamps and don't forget to include a jukebox to get the party started!

MOVIE TIME!

Popcorn at the ready – it's movie time! With a comfy sofa and a big screen, it's like having your own cinema!

LET'S COLOUR!

ADD A SPLASH OF COLOUR TO BRING STEVE TO LIFE!